The Light Through a Hole In The Mirror

Don Schaeffer

ISBN: 978-81-19654-78-9

First Edition: 2024
Rs. 200/-

Cyberwit.net
HIG 45 Kaushambi Kunj, Kalindipuram
Allahabad - 211011 (U.P.) India
http://www.cyberwit.net
Tel: +(91) 9415091004
E-mail: info@cyberwit.net

Printed at Repro India Limited.

Contents

Contents

Eyesight in History

Through the fog
of memory, I still see
the outline of an ordinary story
I am not afraid to tell.
But I am at the edge
of strangeness.
Is it a variation of a
safe and ordinary story
just wrapped in fear
or is it another world?
I am uttering goodbye
to things I used to trust
even as I grip the walls
and cling to the floor.
I can't even see or remember.
My adventure is a new type.
I lose my grip on today
and slide into an history
fantasy.

I saw my face in the mirror

We don't talk
with sound. Our
language is
unspeakable. We are
laced with secrets,
covered with shame.
We cannot be pronounced.

Life forms
in the evening,
during silent times.
Our speech is in
dreams. It goes on
for days, for nights.
It penetrates the dark.

It is still.
It is silent.
Its secrets spread
past the hours.
The stories are
buried in memories.
We don't confess them.

My Brush with Insanity

It's certainly not
as much fun as
the legend suggests.
When you attach
the hallway to the
world of nightmares
to the kitchen door
you simulate it.
It erases all the comforting
memories. It breaks
all the predictable pathways.
It leaves you hungering for clues.
You watch the faces of friends
like it's the word goodbye.

Anna Karenina The Ballet

Figures come
walking slow,
eyes high, seeing
the future and
living quietly in dreams.

Figures slowly paste
little repairs on their time
until the shock
stops them. Then they
get buried.

You can watch them
fall into a hole in the earth.

There are those who regret it
that she just missed salvation,
by just a couple of smiles
and one quiet caress
that never happened.

The music never stops
and the rhythm aids the walking.

Linda of Dreams

My body is a stop along the way.
I rest here. I catch my breath
that ordinarily runs away.
There is the special intimacy
of being alone here
with all my whispers.

When my motion stops,
surrendered, submitted
to something sweeter but
stronger, I feel her
fabric on my chest.
It's a discovery
I've known all along,
but couldn't confess.

The Place for Value in a World of Fact

(comment on an article by Wolfgang Kohler)

In a previous discussion the subject
of does life imply some kind of awareness came up.
I know it's a kind of taboo subject among scientists
who want to keep their precious distance.
But the subject came up. I don't know
what awareness means really—
it has something to do with a process of
making decisions that aren't based
on simple mechanical rules.
It also has to do with a pattern of using
senses that influences behavior.
It really is hard to define, which is
why people don't try.
What use is awareness anyway?
We can just forget the subject—
but we don't want to and
we are stubborn about it.

Two Sides of the Reality Wall

There is a tiny screen door
near the edge of the second panel:
click it.
What if you are half blind
and can't see it?
What if you can see it
but don't know what to do?
What if the instructions
are murkey and not correct?
I see you out there
waving your arms and
saying goodbye.
And I can't hear you.

Doctor's Visit

When the doctor said,
"You didn't die, Donny.
There will be tomorrow."
I looked at her with glazed eyes.
"This place isn't so great
but it made good children."
The sun was shining.

The Spring was going to start.
I rubbed shoulders with fear
and the contact felt good.
Fear does not have
a cold body. He takes the heat
from the world, but
doesn't leave much.

Please Come

The ghosts
can only sneak up.
They're very hard to spot
from this vantage point
where things don't
see ghosts.

They don't try
to hide but
ghosts can't
will to be seen.
They may want to
grab a place in your
friendly world.

They weep
not because they are ghosts
but because
they are alone.

On a Day Off

It's an unpredictable misery.
Even on a quiet day
when there is no one
to disturb you. A small
switch is turned and the
lights of day flicker and threaten.

How long has it been
since you were scared?
It's a state in decline.
It makes some demands.
You have to be in a priveleged
state of vulnerability.

The future: your rescuer
has to be sleeping or
out visiting. Until
the future decides to return
you have no one to confide in.

There is no state of misery
that compares to when the future
goes away to visit someone
you don't know. And you
just yearn for the grand return.
May the future
come back soon.

The Sin of Love

I was so mad
that she was leaving
and shut me out in the end.

She tried to fool me
but I caught on
and burst into the home
of her last days.

I insisted that she stay
and made such a fuss
she didn't feel she had
to tell the truth.

I left her on that last day
feeling that maybe I prevailed
another argument won.
She grudgingly agreed to live.

But lied.

Applied Sighing

Once in a while
I just say it
to nobody—at least
not a body.

I say
"dear God."
It's a laugh.
Nothing is listening.
I could be committing
a miscreance. It

wouldn't even count as a sin.
It's just in vain,
a useless lonely whine
of mention,

request, pleading
to which all I can expect is a scoff.
It's in useless
wasted time
when I could make
more worthy prayers.

The Part That Isn't Ending

I get to know it.
I mean smears of it
or drops or chunks or
particles of it
spread through time
or make pieces that bump.

Sometimes they seem
to move on their own,
these things. How can I
grasp it? Pressed in lines
they create time.

Lining up in
bits of silence,
bits of vacuum
followed by chunks,

asks, urgings, demands,
summaries of the future.
I wake to it,
not privy to what comes
between in fog or darkness
or dreaming.

When it stops,
maybe it will,
it will not be sleep
and all this
will stop ending.

Anna Karenina

(based on the ballet)

The thing is nearly over.
I haven't even
had a chance to embrace.

The kiss remains uncreated,
too few, faded memories.
And it's nearly over.

Only the dark remains
Unbiased unsmiling
outside the

unprejudiced wall.
How did it slip by,
that sneak of time?

The dancers turn away
and the audience
closes their books.

(Dee Di Di Ditty)

Fictitious Moments Ago

When he died
it was a relief.
There were five
pieces of pain,
filling the gaps
between moments
and then it
let him go.
His body floated away
under the eyes of friends.
Dear God
I said goodbye.

The Doors

We make separate rooms
to ease the transition.
We make practice rooms
so it doesn't startle.

The change is hard enough
without the additional shock.
Let the fright go
away on its own.

At the other
end of the hallway
are the original
magic secrets

to behold and learn,
a quiet entrance.
We stopped
calling it an exit.

Nutcake

I am singing to the dog.
I call him Snoopy
even though that's not the name
his family gave him.
It's an aria by Puccini.
The dog watches me
and doesn't walk away.
The dog looks me in the eyes
with that little glisten.
The dog huddles on the floor
with legs all bent. I hear my song
with borrowed sentiment.
We live on the same planet,
Snoopy and I. It is
a joy.

An Inspiration

God made love
for younger people.
We transform by death
as the hunger dries.
You can't blame youth.
You have to rejoice in it
and try to submit.
God helps you,
stripping you. Throwing
lacey cushions on your eyes.
Be calm. Don't fear.
Give all you own.
Possession is robbery
of the future.

Biology Games

We go to this
mysterious new place.
We bring our memories.
We bring
dreams of things
that never happened,
even impossible things.
We bring
wishes and thoughts
about forbidden acts.
It's a dark place.
We have subtle memories
of long ago.
We meld our
dreams with flesh.
Childhood is wicked.
We take evil with us.
We celebrate the end.

Tears When Music Plays

The key to tears
is wanting, which
stretches into something
grander. Wanting and love
buried under
silence are the keys
to something grander.
And you and I
are capable of that.
We can make that
with just sound and light,
salt and water
and ink.

Preparing for a Mystery

What is not known is
a measure of time away
that will quickly pass.
The days are starting to rush
because I begin to learn the secret.

Here is the darkness to
start clouding my eyes,
The sun is still high,
but old questions have
refreshed themselves

They have a crisper new form.
Old questions have deepened
and come back sharper.
The day will come when
mystery will begin to shout.

Being Lost

I don't know
who protects me
but I am kept
away from danger
if I don't slip out
into the
no longer familiar.

There is a
narrow passage I can
still navigate.
My guide is here
only once a week
and lives outside
the steel curtain.

I breathe fear
when my lungs open.
The world denies
my expulsion.
It is kind.
I was always a coward
but now it counts.
The safest place
is no longer a place.

My journey is
brief.

Ballet on Disk

I may take one out,
take one for tonight.
I have a library of sadness.
And sometimes I'm
in the mood.

From my little space
very close to
the edge of memory
I may open the case
and turn the music up.

A day
filled with dreams
swishes of cloth,
I imagine the touch.
I am a specialist
in the feeling of cloth.

It doesn't comfort me
but it feeds the silence
and generates dreams,
adds to the dreams,
replaces time.

www.ingramcontent.com/pod-product-compliance
Lightning Source LLC
Chambersburg PA
CBHW022205160726
48282CB00024B/330